The Little Book of

THE FOUR PRINCIPLES OF *Self Nurture*

Vicki Hope-Robinson

2018 Four Principles of Self Nurture

Copyright © Vicki Hope-Robinson 2018

To John and Saul,
For opening my heart to loving and being loved,
and continuing to be my teachers!

In today's busy world we can often find ourselves going round in circles, waiting for a moment of space to come along in which we can finally work everything out, get our needs met and at last, relax.

Without a sense of direction that moment rarely arrives and we can find ourselves loaded down with guilt, exhaustion, confusion and resentment. Quite simply - lost

The Four Principles of **Solitude**, **Acceptance**, **Gratitude** and **Nurture Rituals** provide you with a structured path to turn to each day, in order to come home to yourself and connect with the true centre of your being – your heart.

If we are to live and love in a way that supports and takes care of the needs of those we love and those we work with or just meet in our day to day, we need to support and take care of ourselves. Nurturing our hearts and souls allows us to be the best that we have to offer the world.

How to Use This Book

This little book contains 108 reflections
and instructions to bring you back home to
yourself, on the days when you're struggling, and
on the days when you're not! The number 108
is inspired by the 108 beads on a Buddhist mala,
used for chanting mantras as an aid to meditative
practice.

You can open this book at any page and discover
that what your heart needs to hear is written in
front of you.

Or you can work your way through the book from front to back, taking a simple reflection as a theme for each day.

This book is about love. Plain and simple. Discovering the one true thing – our heart's capacity to love – there's plenty to go round!

Enjoy!,

Love, Vicki xx

SOLITUDE

Continuously putting off until tomorrow the moment that you pause to take care of yourself will only end in you being resentful and empty. Take some time for yourself today

Are you avoiding Solitude through fear? Be gentle and wrap yourself in comfort if the idea of being alone with yourself is scary

♥

Allow yourself to feel all of your feelings instead
of burying them as a heavy weight to carry around

When the noise inside your head gets deafening,
go sit somewhere quiet for ten minutes.
Come home to your self

What would you really like to know about yourself? Allow time for Solitude and contemplation in order to discover magic about yourself. Start today!

♥

We are all wise. Wisdom is not knowledge. It is seeing what is already there. Be still, breathe and notice what you did not see before

Take a moment to close your eyes and focus on your heart. Any answers you have been seeking will come from here.

♥

Learning to love yourself is the first step to recognising heartfelt love in yourself for others and receiving the love that returns

♥

Being in nature is a direct way of connecting with yourself. Go outside today and make that connection

If you can find a home in your heart, you can find peace anywhere

The wish to be understood is such a natural part of being human. Through Solitude we can slowly begin to understand and know ourselves

♥

The busier you get and the more stressed, the more important it is to step back, breathe and take a moment alone for yourself

The way to "deal with" our emotions is to stay with them. Pay some attention to your feelings today

♥

Each time you face a difficult task, stop before you start and ask yourself are you prepared to commit? Support yourself with commitment

♥

If you listen hard enough you will hear your own truth, take time to tune in

♥

Recognise that you are an integral piece of the jigsaw that makes up the whole universe

♥

The only experience you will ever truly know is right now, this very moment. Notice your breath and savour being alive

♥

When the rain blocks your path, turn back, this may be a message for you to return inside. Take the opportunity to spend some time going within, look for the sun within your heart

♥

If you are one of life's seekers, look no further.
You arrive at your destination every moment,
right here, your self is right here. Welcome!

Let your heart be your guide – without it you are lost

When you find yourself rushing, slow down and breathe, notice what feelings you may be avoiding experiencing – it's time to pay them some attention

When the penny finally drops that the happiness you seek lies within, it's like a million fairy lights turning on! Don't give up – the switch is already there!

♥

It is the subtle doubts that have the most power over us. Sit quietly and allow awareness to reveal your doubts. Let them go

♥

Happiness lies not "out there". It lies "in here".
Place your hand on your heart and breathe deeply
into trusting this truth

♥

When you make time to be with yourself, you can discover the dreams you are hiding from and start building the path to making them reality

♥

You're never alone when you're with your self

♥

Come home to yourself today. Stop, pause for
a moment and breathe. Smile and say
"Welcome Home!"

♥

ACCEPTANCE

There is no wrong choice or wrong path. There is only ever the path you are on. Relax into it . . .

Leave judgement and criticism outside the room –
experience the peace of Acceptance

Sometimes, procrastination can be part of moving forward. Don't be hard on yourself, maybe you need a bit of a run up before taking the jump

All of your feelings are valid

Some days the well will just be dry. As you practice patience, the rain will trickle down from the mountainside and the levels will begin to rise again

When the waves are crashing and clouds scurry across your sky, hold fast to the knowledge that the sun is always shining in your heart

The seams of gold lie in the difficulties we face up to, don't be afraid, the light is through the tunnel. Enter with confidence

Forgive your first reaction, it's your recovery time that counts!

Every moment is an opportunity to start again

If you are panicking at too many things to do today, step back and consider two things that are a priority. Commit to those, and let go

Sometimes we may need to let go of things in order to create a space for something better to arrive in their place

When you are struggling, imagine wringing out a wet cloth, squeezing tight. Then imagine the cloth blowing in the wind. Let go

Life's journeys are littered with obstacles. As you
overcome each one, you gain wisdom and light.
Don't shy away, grasp the opportunity

There is only ever right now, let go of the past.
Treat each moment as an opportunity for a
fresh start

In its imperfection, everything is perfect,
just as it is

If you harm someone or something by accident
remember to be gentle with yourself and forgive.
Guilty ravings will only keep you stuck.

Everything changes. True contentment with this life lies with Acceptance of impermanence – the tide comes in then goes out, then comes in again

When it's cold outside we wrap up warm.
When our emotional world feels very cold, it's
equally important to warm our souls with nurture

Trusting when life is going well is easy. Trusting
when life is difficult is essential

Don't be afraid of going back to the beginning. The beginning is where we start from and also where we end. Don't ever think it's too late to start again

Forgiveness brings power to your life. You need to start with yourself, notice, then begin to let go of all those self-critical thoughts

A sense of anxiety is not always fear of something.
It may just be adrenaline pumping at the
experience of joy and excitement!

When you find yourself obsessively seeking perfection, you are constantly telling yourself you're not good enough. You are. Let go

Our basic nature is natural goodness. Our search in life is to find our way home to that. Remember what you are searching for is here!

When a task seems daunting, let go of the end and just focus on the beginning

Let go of trying too hard to get it right. You might
be surprised by the results

When you hit a wall, step back, don't turn away. Just rest and remain at a distance. Perspective will dawn when you are ready

GRATITUDE

Before rising tomorrow morning list in your head five things you are grateful for. However small. Consider making this a daily practice by creating a Gratitude journal

Enjoy this moment, you will never have it again!

Whenever you hear the rain, think of it as watering your soul

When you reach the top of the mountain,
remember to stop and enjoy the view

Life is impermanence. Be sure to tell those you
love, today and every day, how you feel

If you see the blessings you have in life, don't be guilty, be grateful

When the sun is shining overhead take a moment
to consider someone else may be standing in the
rain. Keep your heart open

In times of great difficulty or frustration, if you can find the courage to practice Gratitude, clarity and a way forward will open up. It's time to trust

As you learn to appreciate beauty in the smallest
of things you travel on the road to your heart.
Get out in nature soon, look around you

When you practice gratitude with others, the river
begins to flow — notice what happens the next
time you say thank you with a smile

When the sky is grey and cloudy, always remember the sun is waiting behind

You may be waiting for a lifetime if you put off happiness and joy "until" you arrive, achieve, obtain or experience something! Look around at where you are, what you have and what you are experiencing right now

You are more than worthy of compassion for yourself. By discovering its true meaning, you automatically share it with those around you

Close your eyes and picture something beautiful.
Smile!

Look around you and appreciate everything in
your life right now – don't wait for something to
be gone before you appreciate it by its absence

Doing something nice today? Remember to stay
in the present and appreciate each moment as
it happens

Make a plan to cut or buy some flowers.
Take a moment to really look closely. Allow
yourself to delight in nature's miraculous beauty

When it's cold outside look inside your heart for extra warmth — it's there, all you have to do is look!

Practicing Gratitude can shed light on the darkest of days. Gratitude for something, however small, can remind us abundance exists

Nature is available to each and every one of us . . .
and it's free! Take a breath!

When you want to think about what's coming next, stop for a moment and notice what is happening right now

The days when nothing special is happening are just as important as all those diary days with big stars on. Appreciate every moment

Savour every second

Instead of worrying about how far you have to go,
celebrate how far you have come!

The sun will always rise again tomorrow

Write a touchstones list – start with five things;
sunshine, dew on early morning grass, butterflies,
a smile from a stranger, the smell of freshly mown
grass. Keep the list close by

Dreams can come true!

NURTURE RITUALS

Love yourself first, loving others will come
naturally and love will follow you wherever you go

What nurturing thing are you doing for yourself today? Make sure there is at least one thing

Each time you light a candle you can allow
yourself to connect with the everlasting light that
burns in your own heart

No matter how loud the voices telling you there
isn't time for you to be important . . . YOU ARE!!
Give yourself a moment today

If anything is going to make sense to you, or you are to find the answers you seek, you must nurture your own heart first

When fear is crippling you into inaction, use a gentle treat as a crutch

Life's too short to spend reading a book you don't enjoy. Put it down!

When it's cold outside we wrap up warm. When our emotional world feels very cold, it's equally important to warm our souls with nurture

Get into your body and out of your mind. Move your body today – walk and notice your physical sensations, let go of your thoughts

On the Four Principles path we are always a work in progress. Give yourself a break – just keep nurturing!

The first time you ask what you really wish for,
you may find yourself blanking out quite quickly.
Don't give up – notice that. Try again

The need for gentleness with ourselves is a lifetime commitment. Start today. Notice how fast you are going, breathe and slow down

Asking for support is not a sign of weakness.
It is a sign of wisdom

Treat yourself. Especially if you think you don't
deserve it

If you are feeling low and you are alone, give yourself a virtual hug. Wrap yourself in a blanket — if you don't have one, buy one!

Rushing around we trip or stub our toe. What are
we avoiding? Often painful feelings. Don't wait
to stub your toe before realising you need love.
Treat yourself to a nurture ritual now

You may be shocked to discover the level of
nurturing you may need to perform before you
begin to pierce the armour that shields your heart

When you are trying to change, and it's tough, remember to nurture, nurture, nurture — little treats on a regular basis. Find your heart

Do you have a dream? Follow it, it will lead you to bright places beyond imagination

Sprinkle some fairy dust on your day today. Allow yourself to suspend the limitations on what you do – and do something new and different!

When you 'lighten up' the way forward becomes
'lit up'!

When the sun is shining outside and you have to work inside, bring some sunshine in – pick some flowers for your workspace

We find the courage to face the difficult things in life, not by pushing ourselves hard, but by being very gentle and nurturing ourselves

We all need love. We all need nurture.
Learning to give ourselves these things is the path
to learning to love and nurture others honestly,
without conditions

When you see a part of yourself you don't like,
don't turn away. Be compassionate to yourself.
Give yourself a gift

No matter how much you have treated yourself, relaxed and nurtured – if your heart tells you it needs more, give it, have it

Never stop nurturing. It's a job for life!

To continue the journey . . .

Instagram – thefourprinciplesofselfnurture
Facebook – thefourprinciplesofselfnurture
Twitter - @fourprinciples

vicki@thefourprinciples.co.uk
www.thefourprinciples.co.uk

Printed in Great Britain
by Amazon